Global Warming

Chris Oxlade

FRANKLIN WATTS
LONDON•SYDNEY

© 2002 Franklin Watts

First published in 2002 by
Franklin Watts
96 Leonard Street
London
EC2A 4XD

Franklin Watts Australia
56 O'Riordan Street
Alexandria
NSW 2015

ISBN: 0 7496 4480 X
Dewey Decimal Classification 333.7
A CIP catalogue reference for this book is available
from the British Library

Printed in Dubai

Editor: Kate Banham
Designer: Mark Mills
Art Direction: Jonathan Hair

Illustration: Ian Thompson
Picture Research: Diana Morris
Consultant: Sally Morgan, Ecoscene

Acknowledgements
The publishers would like to thank the following for permission to
reproduce photographs in this book.
Toshiyuki Aizawal/Reuters/Popperfoto: 29t; Jim Amos/SPL: 16t; Klaus
Andrews/Still Pictures: 4tr, 15bl; Alex Bartel/Ecoscene: 26t; Alian Compost/
Still Pictures: 8t; Anthony Cooper/Ecoscene: 21b, 27bl; DERA/Still Pictures:
7cl; Digital Vision: front cover, 10-11b, 12, 16b, 23c, 25t, 28b; David Drain/Still
Pictures: 4bl; Ecoscene: 11t; Mark Edwards/Still Pictures: 13c, 27br; Chris
Fairclough: 5b, 15cr; Peter Frischmut/Still Pictures: 22b; Pierre Gleizes/Still
Pictures: 21t; Richard Glover/Ecoscene: 7b, 11b; Angela Hampton/Ecoscene:
23b; Andy Hibbert/Ecoscene: 16b; David Hoffman/Environmental Picture
Library: 19t; Graham Kitching/Ecoscene: 5c; Harvey Lloyd/Still Pictures: 24-
25b; Vanessa Miles/Environmental Images: 13b; Hank Morgan/SPL: 14b, 20c;
NASA/SPL:9t, 23t; Novosti/SPL: 17t; Popperfoto: 29t, 29b; John Sanford/SPL:
19b; Kevin Schafer/Still Pictures: 27t; Francois Suchel/Still Pictures: 8b;
Alan Towse/Ecoscene: 14t; Eileen Tweedy/Guildhall Library/Art Archive: 15t;
Albert Visage/Still Pictures: 24t.

Contents

Words printed in *italics* are explained in the glossary.

About global warming

Storms, droughts, coastal flooding, famine, habitat destruction... The planet as we know it will be in increasing peril over the next few decades from these natural disasters if we do not act to reduce what scientists call *global warming*.

What is global warming?

Global warming is an increase in the temperature of the Earth's *atmosphere*. Weather records show that during the 20th century, the atmosphere warmed by just over 0.5° C. This warming is predicted to continue. Scientists think that global warming is caused by gases produced mainly by people burning *fossil fuels* such as coal and oil. The gases are trapping heat from the Sun in our atmosphere. One of these gases is *carbon dioxide*.

Industry pours a huge amount of carbon dioxide into the atmosphere.

In 50 years olives may no longer grow here owing to climate change caused by global warming.

Climate change

You might think that a slightly warmer atmosphere would not be a problem. In fact, in colder countries, it could be an advantage! But the main effect of global warming will be a change in the world's weather, with some disastrous effects. The patterns of weather (called *climates*) that places on Earth get every year will change. This is known as *climate change*.

Fifty years from now

If global warming carries on, what will the world be like in 50 years' time, in the middle of the 21st century? *Climatologists* (scientists who study climates) think that the atmosphere will have warmed by at least another degree Celsius. Patterns of sunshine, rainfall and storms will change. Climate changes will alter how plants and crops grow, affecting our food supplies. The sea level will also rise, leading to more flooding along low-lying coasts.

It's not too late

Most scientists agree that global warming is happening, and that we are causing it by our activities on Earth. They also agree that we can stop and even reverse global warming over the next few decades if we reduce the amount of gases we put into the atmosphere. We can all help to achieve this.

One of the predicted effects of global warming is an increase in rainfall in some areas. This may cause floods.

◆ How you can help

Car engines, which burn petrol or diesel fuel, are one of the main producers of the gases that cause global warming. So a very simple way to help reduce global warming is to walk or ride a bicycle instead of getting a lift by car.

Walk or cycle to school and save the planet!

The atmosphere and the weather

Global warming happens in the Earth's atmosphere. The atmosphere is like a blanket of air that surrounds the Earth. Air is constantly swirling around, and this creates the weather that we experience from day to day.

Atmospheric layers

Compared to the size of the Earth, the atmosphere is very shallow. You can think of it as being like the skin on an apple. The atmosphere has no definite end. Instead, it gradually gets thinner and thinner, until it eventually fades into space, about 300 kilometres above the Earth's surface. Meteorologists divide the atmosphere into several different layers (see diagram). The weather happens in the lowest level of the atmosphere, called the troposphere.

Gases in the air

The air in the atmosphere is actually a mixture of many different gases. It is mainly made up of nitrogen (79%) and oxygen (20%). Most of the remaining 1% is a gas called argon. The last 0.1% is made up of many different gases, including carbon dioxide, which makes up about 0.035% of the air. The air also contains some water vapour (water in gas form).

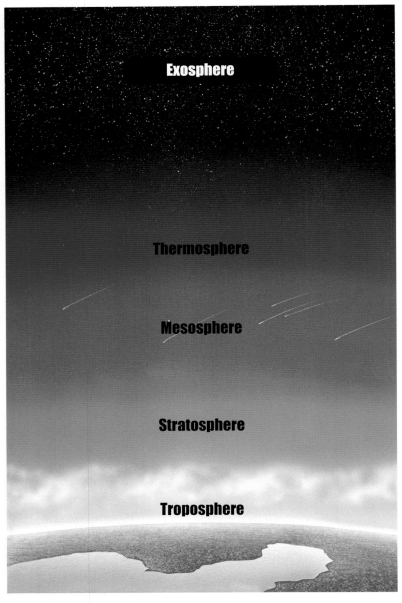

Exosphere

Thermosphere

Mesosphere

Stratosphere

Troposphere

The layers of the Earth's atmosphere.

Driving the weather

All the energy that drives the world's weather comes from the Sun. But the Sun's energy heats different parts of the Earth's surface by different amounts. The tropics are heated more than the poles. The land heats up and cools down more quickly than the oceans, but the oceans store heat for much longer than the land. The land and oceans heat the air above them. This means that the air in some parts of the atmosphere gets warmer than the air in other parts. This causes the air to swirl about, creating winds.

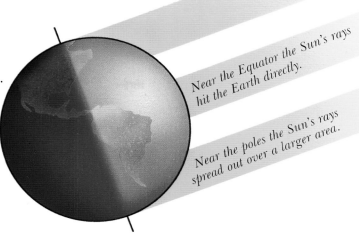

Near the Equator the Sun's rays hit the Earth directly.

Near the poles the Sun's rays spread out over a larger area.

The Sun's rays spread out more the further you go from the Equator, so their heat is also spread out.

Swirls of cloud show weather systems caused by the uneven way in which the Sun heats the Earth.

◆ Science in action

This experiment shows how different types of land cover, such as snow and dark soil, absorb different amounts of light from the Sun, and have different effects on the air above. This is called the 'albedo' effect.

You will need: 2 pieces of card, one white and one black.

Place both pieces of card in the sunshine. After a few minutes feel both. Is one warmer than the other?

What is a climate?

Climate is the general pattern of weather that a place has over a long period of time. Although the weather in a particular place can change quite dramatically from day to day, the climate stays the same from year to year. For example, a temperate climate has dry, warm summers and cool, wet winters, even though it can rain one day and be dry the next at any time of the year.

A tropical climate is hot all year round, with heavy rain nearly every day.

The greenhouse effect

The Sun provides the heat that keeps the Earth warm.

If you have been inside a greenhouse, you'll know that when the Sun shines it gets warmer inside than outside. This is because the greenhouse glass traps heat energy. Energy from the Sun goes through the glass, but heat from inside cannot get out. In a similar way, the Earth's atmosphere traps energy from the Sun. This is known as the *greenhouse effect*.

Energy in . . .

The Sun gives out rays of energy called radiation. The radiation travels through space at the speed of light (300,000 kilometres per second) and reaches the Earth eight minutes later. We see some of the radiation as light. The rest is made up of some heat and some ultra-violet light. About a third of the radiation is reflected back into space by clouds. Some is absorbed by the atmosphere, heating it slightly. Some more is reflected back into space by the Earth's surface. The rest is absorbed by the surface, and heats it up.

Clouds reflect radiation back into space.
More cloud cover reduces the greenhouse effect.

. . . and energy out

The warmed surface of the Earth emits the energy back into the atmosphere, but in the form of heat energy called infra-red radiation, and none as light. In effect, the surface changes the energy from light to heat. Most of this infra-red radiation escapes into space, but some of it is absorbed by gases in the atmosphere, known as *greenhouse gases*. This means that the heat is taken up by the atmosphere, making it warmer.

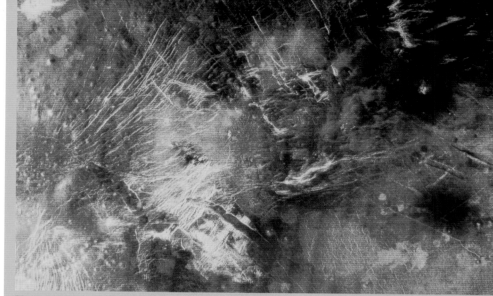

This radar image shows the surface of Venus. Here the greenhouse effect has run away with itself. The surface temperature is 480°C.

Earth's atmosphere, containing greenhouse gases

heat from the Sun

Some heat is trapped in the Earth's atmosphere, instead of escaping into space.

◆ Science in action

This simple greenhouse model traps heat in a similar way to the atmosphere.

You will need: cardboard box, black paint, transparent plastic food wrap, pen, thermometer

Paint the inside of the cardboard box black (or line it with black paper). Cover the top with the plastic food wrap. With a pen, pierce a hole in the side. Stand the box outside in the sunshine. After half an hour, measure the temperature inside and outside the box.

Hot and cold

The greenhouse effect traps heat, and the swirling air in the atmosphere spreads the heat around the world. If there were no greenhouse effect, heat from the Earth's surface would escape straight into space without warming the atmosphere. The Earth would be much colder, almost covered in ice, and probably lifeless.

A natural balance

The greenhouse effect is often thought to be caused only by human activities. But it is a natural process that has been going on for thousands of millions of years. The greenhouse effect traps heat in the atmosphere, but only temporarily. Overall, the same amount of energy escapes as comes from the Sun. So the average temperature of the atmosphere stays the same.

Greenhouse gases

The gases that absorb heat in the atmosphere are known as greenhouse gases. They make up less than 0.1% of the atmosphere. Some are natural and some come from human activities.

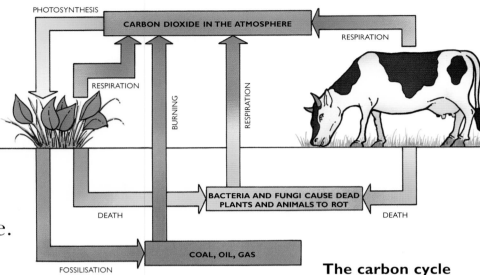

The carbon cycle

Carbon dioxide is taken from the atmosphere by green plants and returned to the atmosphere by animal *respiration* and the rotting of dead matter.

Here you can find out about the greenhouse gases that occur naturally and where they come from.

Carbon dioxide

Carbon dioxide is one of the main greenhouse gases. It is made up of the chemical elements carbon and oxygen. Carbon dioxide makes up about 0.035% of the atmosphere. This percentage is often written down as 350 parts per million (*ppm*), meaning that there are 350 carbon dioxide molecules in every million molecules of gas in the air.

The carbon cycle

All the complex chemicals that make up plants, animals and other organisms (such as fungi) contain strings of carbon atoms. Carbon is constantly moving between animals and plants, the land and oceans, and the atmosphere, where it is contained in carbon dioxide. As part of the carbon cycle, carbon dioxide is constantly being put into the atmosphere and taken out of the atmosphere.

Rainforests take in and give out more carbon dioxide than any other *ecosystem*.

How carbon moves around

Plants and animals give out carbon dioxide when they respire. Carbon dioxide is also taken in by plants when they produce food by photosynthesis. When plants and animals die, their parts are broken down by *decomposers* such as bacteria and fungi. The decomposers release carbon dioxide into the air. The oceans also take in and give out carbon dioxide.

More greenhouse gases

Water vapour, which enters the atmosphere when water *evaporates* from soil, plants and oceans, is the gas that is most responsible for the natural greenhouse effect. *Ozone*, which is a form of oxygen that occurs at some levels of the atmosphere, is another greenhouse gas. The other natural greenhouse gases are methane and nitrous oxide. Methane is produced by animals such as termites and cattle, and comes from swamps. Nitrous oxide comes from rotting vegetation.

The carbon that came from the atmosphere when this tree grew is now returning to the atmosphere as it rots.

◆ Sustainable solution

Reforestation in Kaingaroa Forest, New Zealand.

As plants grow, they take in carbon dioxide from the atmosphere to make food. The carbon from the carbon dioxide is used to build the substances that make up the plant. Planting new trees in places where forests have been cut down will help to remove excess carbon dioxide from the air. This is called reforestation.

Upsetting the balance

Every day hundreds of millions of cars put carbon dioxide into the atmosphere.

Ever since the Industrial Revolution began in Europe in the middle of the 18th century, humans have been adding extra greenhouse gases to the atmosphere. This has upset the natural balance of greenhouse gases, creating an increase in the greenhouse effect, which is causing global warming.

Carbon dioxide from fuels

We are adding huge amounts of carbon dioxide to the atmosphere by burning fossil fuels (coal, gas and oil) in cars, factories and power stations. Carbon dioxide is made when these fuels are burned. In the developed world, each person's energy use is responsible for putting about 10 tonnes of carbon dioxide into the atmosphere every year.

Carbon dioxide from forests

The cutting down, or deforestation, of the world's rainforests is also adding carbon dioxide to the atmosphere. When the forest is cleared for farming or ranching, most of the vegetation is burned or rots away. This releases carbon dioxide into the atmosphere. Normally the forest cannot re-grow, so the carbon dioxide cannot be taken back in by new plants.

Slash-and-burn farming destroys the fragile forest soil, preventing re-growth of the forest.

Carbon dioxide in the atmosphere

About a third of the carbon dioxide that goes into the atmosphere because of human activities is soaked up by the oceans and by plants. But the rest stays in the atmosphere. At the present rate, there will be more than 700 ppm of carbon dioxide in the atmosphere by 2100. That's double what it is now, and three times the level before the Industrial Revolution.

Old refrigerators contain **CFCs** which can be released when the fridge is thrown away.

Particles in the air

Not all the pollutants we put into the atmosphere add to the greenhouse effect. Microscopic particles of solids and liquids created by burning fuels, by agriculture and by industry, actually reflect energy from the Sun, reducing the greenhouse effect.

Sources of other gases

The amount of methane in the atmosphere more than doubled in the 20th century, mainly owing to cattle ranching and rice growing, which both create methane. Nitrous oxide has also increased because of agriculture and chemical industries. We have also added gases called chlorofluorocarbons (*CFCs*), which were used widely in spray cans, fridges and air-conditioners until the 1990s. They add to the greenhouse effect. Other polluting gases, such as sulphur dioxide, react chemically with the air to produce more ozone in the lower atmosphere.

◆ How you can help

Every time you boil water in a kettle or turn on a light you are using electricity that has probably been produced by burning fossil fuels in power stations. If you only boil as much water as you need, and turn lights off when they are not needed, less carbon dioxide will go into the atmosphere. You can also buy energy-efficient light bulbs which use a fraction of the energy of ordinary light bulbs.

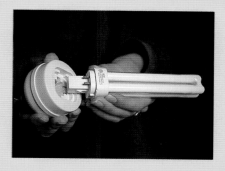

Energy-efficient light bulbs help to reduce global warming.

Gathering evidence

The news media, newspapers and books give lots of facts and figures about the greenhouse effect, global warming and climate change. But where does this information come from? How do we know what the climate was like ten years ago, a hundred years ago, and even millions of years ago?

Measuring the weather

Every day *meteorological* organisations in every country of the world monitor the weather. They measure temperature, rainfall, wind speed and direction, air pressure, sunshine, and the type and number of clouds. Meteorologists use the data to produce weather forecasts. The data is also stored as a record of the past weather, and used to investigate possible climate change.

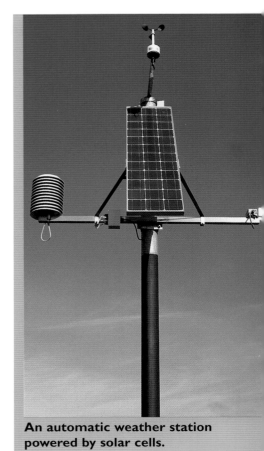

An automatic weather station powered by solar cells.

Computers are perfect machines for storing the huge amount of weather data that is collected every day.

Climate clues

It is not just the weather that provides evidence for global warming and climate change. Climatologists make many other observations and measurements, often using data from remote-sensing satellites. For example, they record ocean temperatures and currents, the area of snow cover, the extent of sea ice at the poles, the length of glaciers, and changing vegetation patterns.

This scene of the frozen River Thames in London painted in 1814 shows that winters were much colder then than now.

Weather records

Many megabytes of data from thousands of weather stations are stored every day to create weather records. But we only have accurate weather records for the years since 1861, when organised recording began. However, we can get an idea of what climates were like for a few hundred years before this from historical documents.

The distant past

To find out what climates were like thousands or millions of years ago, we have to look at things that were formed at the time, such as fossils. Fossils tell us what sort of animals and plants were living in a certain place at a certain time. By comparing where similar animals and plants live today, we can work out what the climate was like.

◆ Science in action

Nature is often a good guide to how climate has changed. Trees grow better in warmer, sunnier years than colder, more cloudy years. Try measuring the tree rings of a cut log. There is a ring for each year of growth. Wider rings show more growth in that year, indicating that the weather was warmer.

Analysing bubbles of gas in ice deep under the ice cap shows us what the atmosphere was like thousands of years ago.

Changing climates

Remember that climate is the overall pattern of weather that a place has over a long period of time. One of main effects of global warming is that climates around the world are beginning to change slightly. But changing climates are not a new thing.

Temperature changes

The Earth has experienced many cycles of warming and cooling since it was formed more than four thousand million years ago. For example, one hundred million years ago during the *Cretaceous* period, the *average global temperature* was about 10°C higher than it is today. Dinosaurs lived in forests at the south pole, and much of the land we live on today was under the tropical sea.

When this dinosaur died the world's overall temperature was far warmer than today.

Today, very few things live at the south pole – only hardy animals such as penguins and seals. Once, however, it was home to forests and dinosaurs.

Periods of cold

Ice ages were periods up to 100,000 years long when the average global temperature was a few degrees lower than it is today. The ice caps that now cover the poles extended over northern Europe, North America, South America and Australia. The last ice age ended only about 10,000 years ago. There's no reason to think that there won't be another ice age in the next few thousand years.

Mammoths found in frozen ground today lived during the last ice age.

Recent climate change

Weather records show that global warming is happening. The average global temperature (which is about 15°C) increased by about 0.6°C during the 20th century. Overall, the 1990s were the warmest decade since weather records began, and 1998 was the warmest year ever.

More evidence for global warming

A study of photographs taken from satellites shows that snow cover across the world has reduced by about 10% since the 1960s. Glaciers in the world's high mountain ranges are shrinking back by a few metres a year. Arctic sea ice has reduced by about 10% since the 1950s, and in 1995 a massive iceberg 36 kilometres by 75 kilometres, and 200 metres thick, broke off from Antarctica. Sea levels rose by between 10 and 25 centimetres in the 20th century.

This chart shows how the average global temperature has changed over the last 100 years.

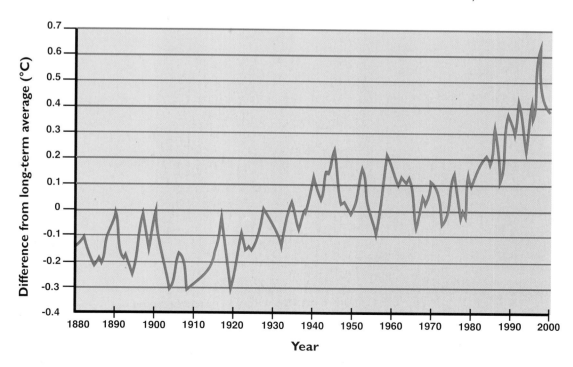

More causes of climate change

Most scientists agree that climates around the world appear to be changing. But the greenhouse effect and global warming are not necessarily the cause of all climate changes. So what other factors can affect the climate?

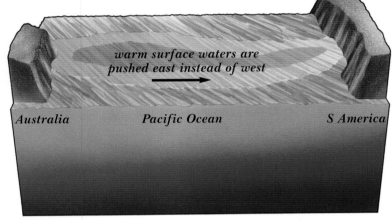

warm water evaporates producing storm clouds

warm surface waters are pushed east instead of west

Australia　　*Pacific Ocean*　　*S America*

El Niño

El Niño (pronounced 'el nee nyo') is a natural event that happens every few years. During an El Niño event, which lasts for about 12–18 months, the ocean currents in the Pacific Ocean near South America change direction, bringing to the surface water that is warmer than normal. This affects the climate in the area and also globally. The 1997–98 event is thought to have caused severe storms and floods in Peru, crop failures in East Africa, huge forest fires in Indonesia, and thousands of deaths. Climatologists do not yet understand how or why El Niño happens.

The impact of a huge meteor would throw enough dust into the atmosphere to reduce global temperatures for years.

Catastrophic events

Events such as volcanic eruptions and meteor impacts also cause climate change by sending large amounts of dust into the atmosphere. For example, when Mount Pinatubo in the Philippines erupted violently in 1991, a vast cloud of ash and droplets of acid rose 40,000 metres into the atmosphere and spread slowly around the world. This reflected some of the Sun's energy back into space. Global temperatures dropped by 0.5°C for more than a year.

Logging destroys large areas of rainforest, causing local climate change.

Changing land use

Human activities on the land can also change the climate. Altering the amount of vegetation changes how much energy is reflected and absorbed by the land. This can affect the temperature, how clouds form, and how much rain falls as well. For example, it is thought that cutting down the rainforests will reduce the amount of water that goes back into the air from the forests, so reducing the amount of rainfall.

Space cycles

Long-term climate changes are thought to be caused by cycles in the movement of the Earth and the Sun's activity. One theory is that the ice ages are caused by the fact that the Earth wobbles slightly on its axis over thousands of years, which changes how heat spreads over the surface.

Sunspots

Sunspots are cool areas on the surface of the Sun. Between 1645 and 1715 there were almost no sunspots. At the same time the European climate turned colder.

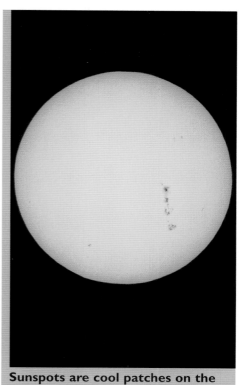

Sunspots are cool patches on the surface of the Sun.

19

Modelling the future

We have a good idea about what has happened to the climate in the past. You might have heard predictions about what is going to happen to climates in the future. How do climatologists make these predictions?

This researcher is testing a model to predict climate changes caused by the greenhouse effect.

Climate computer models

The way the greenhouse effect works, how it creates global warming and how climates are affected is amazingly complicated. To try to predict what will happen in the future, climatologists use complex computer programs. The programs are called general circulation models (GCMs). They are mathematical models of the atmosphere. Even on powerful super computers, the programs take hours or even days to come up with their answers.

How hot could it get?

Climatologists give their *climate models* data about how much of each greenhouse gas we are likely to pump into the atmosphere every year, and ask them to predict what climates will be like up to a hundred years into the future. The latest models predict that the global average temperature at the Earth's surface will rise by between 1.5 and 5.8°C by 2100.

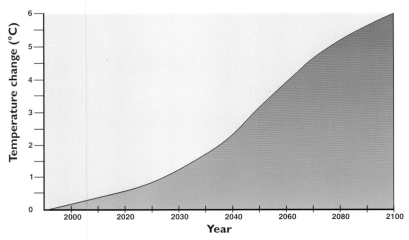

Over the 21st century Earth's average temperature could rise by as much as 5.8°C.

Model problems

Computer climate models can only do the calculations that climatologists ask them to do. If the atmosphere works in a slightly different way to how the scientists think it does, their models will give the wrong answers. For example, at the moment climatologists don't completely understand what effect clouds have on global warming, or exactly how much carbon dioxide the oceans will soak up.

Different views

You will have heard different views about the seriousness of global warming from different people and organisations. Organisations such as oil companies, who sell oil to make money, often say that climatologists have not proved the link between human activities and global warming. Environmental organisations will often quote the worst-case scenario predicted by climatologists.

◆ How you can help

If you feel strongly that we should try to reduce global warming you could support an environmental campaign group such as Greenpeace or Friends of the Earth. You can find addresses for their websites on page 30.

Oil companies tend to play down the effects of global warming.

Effects of global warming

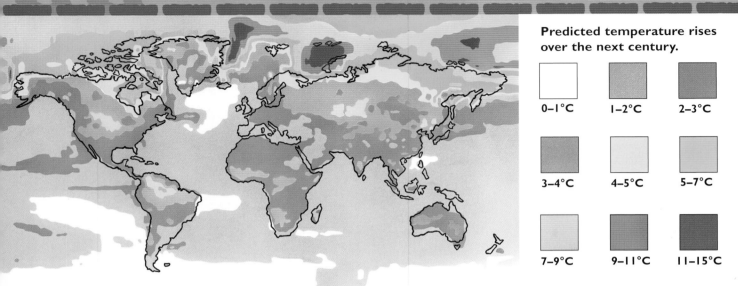

Predicted temperature rises over the next century.

0–1°C	1–2°C	2–3°C
3–4°C	4–5°C	5–7°C
7–9°C	9–11°C	11–15°C

If the global temperature rises by about 3°C by the end of this century, what do climatologists predict will happen to our climates? Global warming will probably affect daily temperatures round the world, change the pattern of rainfall and increase the severity of storms.

Drier and wetter

Climate models predict that, because of global warming, there will be about 5% more rainfall by 2100. But that does not mean it will be wetter everywhere. North America, northern Europe and northern Asia will get more rain, but countries in the tropics will get less. These changing rainfall patterns will mean that rivers will flood more often in winter in some places, but there could be drought in other places.

Hotter and colder

Computer climate models predict a rise in global temperatures of about 3°C. But this is a global average. The temperature will not rise by this amount all over the world. In the world's higher *latitudes*, nearer to the poles, the rise may be more like 5° or 6°C. Towards the Equator the rise may be only 1°C. Overall, that would mean more very hot days and fewer very cold days.

Increased rainfall in Germany has resulted in rivers flooding much more often than previously.

Storms on the way

Winter storms and hurricanes get their energy from the warm oceans. As sea temperatures rise, these storms will be able to gather more energy. Their winds will be stronger and they will carry more rain. This will lead to increased damage from high winds and flooding both inland and on the coast from *storm surges*.

A hurricane system seen from above.

Deserts and forests

Climate change will affect how natural vegetation grows around the world. By the middle of the century, large areas of lush rainforests and tropical grasslands may have turned to dusty deserts because of less rain and rising temperatures. But in the northern hemisphere, forests will actually grow larger because there will be more rain, higher temperatures and more carbon dioxide in the atmosphere. One advantage of this is that the forests will take in some of the carbon dioxide we put into the atmosphere.

Vegetation will find it harder to survive in areas which already receive little rainfall.

◆ How you can help

Recycling is a good way of helping to cut down global warming. Recycling saves not only the materials the goods are made from, but also the energy that would be needed to make brand-new materials. And using energy means burning fossil fuels.

Always try to recycle glass, tins and paper.

Problems for us

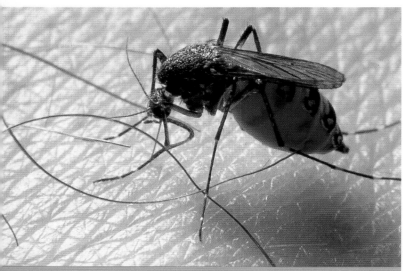

There is already evidence of malaria-carrying mosquitoes spreading to new habitats as climates begin to change.

We know that global warming will create climate changes. But a change in the weather is a minor problem compared to the other problems that global warming and climate change will cause. Humans, animals and plants will all suffer.

Water resources

Changing rainfall patterns will mean that many countries will have less water for drinking and irrigating crops. Unfortunately, most of these countries are ones which are already short of water. By the end of the century, 100 million more people could be short of water. To make matters worse, if the world's population continues to increase as it is doing today, the smaller amount of water will have to be shared out among twice as many people.

Food for thought

Changing temperatures and rainfall patterns will affect how well crops grow. In the tropics, reduced rainfall will reduce the amount of food that can be grown. Further north and south, warmer climates will increase how much food can be grown. But overall, production of important crops such as wheat will fall, leading to increased food prices, and in some countries, millions more people going hungry.

Reduced rainfall as a result of global warming will reduce yields of important crops such as wheat.

Rising sea levels

Climate models predict a rise in sea levels of about 60 centimetres by the end of the century. That does not sound much, but it would put 200 million people living near coasts under threat of flooding, especially in stormy areas. The rise in sea level will be caused by melting ice from ice caps flowing into the oceans, but also because the water in the oceans will expand as it warms. In the distant future, if all the ice in the world melts, sea levels could rise by 65 metres.

Low-lying coastal areas may be flooded so often that they will become uninhabitable.

◆ Science in action

Try this simple experiment to see how water expands as it warms up.

You will need: a plastic bottle, modelling clay, a transparent straw, a marker pen, a bowl

Fill the bottle to the brim with cold water. Mould a blob of modelling clay around the straw. Push the clay into the neck of the bottle to make a seal. Mark the height of the water in the straw. Stand the bottle in a bowl of warm water and watch the water expand up the straw.

Stopping global warming

In most countries using more electricity means burning more coal, oil or gas, and creating more carbon dioxide.

At the beginning of the 21st century, carbon dioxide *emissions* are increasing every year. The predictions about global warming given in this book assume that this will carry on. So, is it possible for us to stop global warming or even to reduce it?

Cutting carbon emissions

The most important action to take to stop global warming is to reduce carbon dioxide emissions. Most carbon dioxide emissions come from burning fossil fuels such as coal, oil and gas in power stations. To stop carbon dioxide levels from rising above 360 ppm, and preventing global warming getting any worse, we would have to reduce emissions by 60% immediately. This is simply impractical at the moment, but we must use electricity and fossil fuels more efficiently so that much less fuel needs to be burned. If we carry on pumping carbon dioxide into the atmosphere at the present rate, there will be more than 700 ppm of carbon dioxide in the atmosphere by 2100.

Renewable energy

One way we can use less fossil fuel in power stations is to make electricity in other ways. Electricity made in some of these ways is known as renewable energy. Examples of renewable energy sources are solar power, wind power, and *hydroelectric* and *tidal power*. All these use energy that originally came from the Sun. In fact, the amount of energy that comes from the Sun is 6,000 times greater than the energy we actually use.

Adapting to change

If climates do change as much as climatologists predict, we will have to take action to prevent damage to properties and people from the increased storms and floods. For example, we will have to build extra *flood barriers* or move people away from low-lying coasts. We will also have to make sure people in the developing countries are able to grow enough food.

Wind farms produce emission-free electricity, but are considered too ugly or noisy by some people.

The Thames Barrier protects low-lying districts of London from tidal surges. It will have to be used more frequently if sea levels rise.

◆Sustainable solution

One form of fuel that will help to reduce global warming is biomass fuel. It comes from burning plants or plant oils. The carbon dioxide they release when they burn is balanced by the carbon dioxide they take in as they grow.

A vehicle powered by biomass fuel.

27

Waking up to global warming

Svante Arrhenius (1859–1927), the first scientist to predict global warning.

The idea of global warming and climate change was first put forward more than 100 years ago by Swedish scientist, Svante Arrhenius. Arrhenius said that the global temperature could rise by a few degrees because of the amount of coal and oil that was being burned. But it was not until the 1980s that scientists began taking the idea seriously.

International efforts

In America the summer of 1988 was extremely hot. Raging wildfires caused millions of dollars of damage and grain production was very poor because of lack of rain. This event was one of the things that persuaded climatologists from many different countries to form the Intergovernmental Panel of Climate Change (IPCC for short). The IPCC is supported by the World Meteorological Organisation.

Frequent wildfires are a result of reducing rainfall.

Talking shops

The first time that the world's governments met to discuss global warming was the Earth Summit of 1992, held in Rio de Janeiro, Brazil. Other conferences followed, including one in Kyoto, Japan, in 1997. Here, the Kyoto Protocol was suggested. It says that carbon dioxide emissions every year should be reduced to a level 5% below the emissions of 1990 by the year 2012. In 2001 in Bern, Germany, 180 countries agreed to the Kyoto Protocol.

Delegates from more than 100 countries attended the climate conference in Kyoto, Japan.

Difficult decisions

The USA has 5% of the world's population, but produces about 20% of the world's greenhouse gases. The USA did not agree to the Kyoto Protocol. Their government is concerned that reducing emissions would mean job losses and loss of freedom for people to use their cars. However, in the latest round of talks, the cuts only affect the top-ranking industrialised nations – called Annex 1 countries. Even China and Russia are exempt. This accounts for some of the reluctance of the USA to make changes when competing nations are excluded.

Final word

There is no doubt that global warming is happening and that it is here to stay. Few climatologists doubt that it is being caused by human activities. But it has taken governments a little longer to be convinced and to react to the problem. Initiatives such as the Kyoto Protocol show that they are now taking measures to address the problem.

In 2001 US President George W. Bush backed out of the Kyoto Protocol.

Further information

There are websites where you can find out more about topics mentioned in this book.

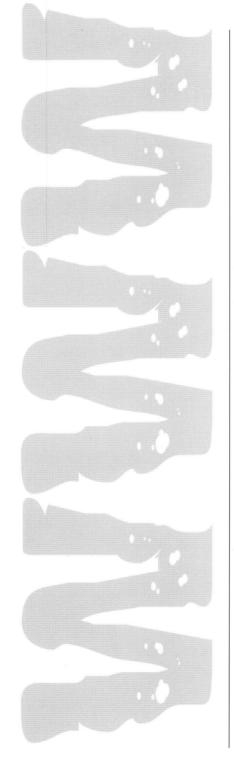

The Meteorological Office in Bracknell, Berkshire UK is the national weather service of the UK. On their website at **www.met-office. gov.uk** you can find forecasts, maps and general weather information.

Another weather website is **www.royal-met-soc.org.uk**. This is the website of the Royal Meteorological Society – an organisation for weather experts and enthusiasts.

For the latest news on climate change visit the website of the World Meteorological Organisation at **www.wmo.ch**. Here you will also find details of the Intergovernmental Panel on Climate Change.

The National Oceanic and Atmospheric Administration (NOAA) is the national weather forecasting service of the USA. Visit their website at **www.nws.noaa.gov** for forecasts and maps which you can download.

The national weather service of Australia is the Australian Bureau of Meteorology. For forecasts, maps and more general information, check out their website at **bom.gov.au**.

The Environment Australia website **www.ea.gov.au** offers up-to-date information on the latest environmental research and initiatives. There are pages on many different topics including the greenhouse effect and pollution.

For general environmental information, check out Friends of the Earth, an organisation that campaigns worldwide to protect the environment. Their website is at **www.foe.co.uk**.

You can also visit the Greenpeace website at **www.greenpeace.co.uk** for environmental information. To find out about the organisation's environmental campaigns in Australia, check out **www.greenpeace.org.au**.

Glossary

Atmosphere
Layer of air that covers the Earth like a thick blanket.

Average global temperature
Average temperature of the atmosphere all over the world.

Carbon dioxide
Gas made up of carbon and oxygen. It is the most important greenhouse gas.

CFC
Short for chlorofluoro-carbon, a type of chemical that destroys ozone in the atmosphere.

Climate change
Gradual change in the world's climates over time.

Climate model
Complex computer program that simulates what will happen to the world's climate over several decades.

Climate
Pattern of weather at a place over a long period of time.

Climatologist
Scientist who studies climates, climate change and global warming.

Cretaceous
Period in geological time that lasted from 145 million years ago to 65 million years ago.

Decomposer
Something that breaks dead matter down into more simple chemicals.

Emissions
Chemicals emitted from engines or power stations.

Ecosystem
The way plants and animals in a particular area interact with their environment.

Evaporation
Change from liquid to gas at a temperature lower than the liquid's boiling point.

Flood barrier
Structure like a dam that prevents water from flowing inland along a river.

Fossil fuel
Fuel formed from the remains of ancient animals and plants that died millions of years ago. Coal, oil and gas are fossil fuels.

Global warming
Gradual increase in the average global temperature of the Earth's atmosphere.

Greenhouse effect
The way in which the Earth's atmosphere traps heat from the Sun.

Greenhouse gas
One of several gases that trap heat and that are responsible for the greenhouse effect.

Hydroelectric power
Electricity made using the energy in flowing water.

Latitude
Distance to the north or south of the equator, measured in degrees. Low latitudes are near the equator. High latitudes are near the poles.

Meteorology
The study of the weather.

Ozone
Form of oxygen that occurs at some levels of the atmosphere. The greatest concentration of ozone occurs high in the stratosphere.

ppm
Short for parts per million, a way of measuring the amount of a substance in a mixture.

Respiration
The chemical processes in a cell that use oxygen and release carbon dioxide and energy.

Storm surge
Increase in sea level under an area of low pressure in the atmosphere, such as an Atlantic low or a hurricane.

Tidal power
Electricity made using the energy in rising and falling tides.

Index